quintessence

*the poetry
of true nature*

sara priestley

RIVER GROVE
BOOKS

Published by River Grove Books
Austin, TX
www.rivergrovebooks.com

Distributed by River Grove Books

Design and composition by Greenleaf Book Group
Cover design by Greenleaf Book Group
Cover image: Abstract background, ©iStockphoto.com/lmuse

Publisher's Cataloging-in-Publication data is available.

Print ISBN: 978-1-63299-217-8

eBook ISBN: 978-1-63299-218-5

First Edition

For my fellow explorers of true nature,

As my friend and mentor, Garret Kramer, says,
"While sometimes a brief echo, everyone's experienced the inkling
that things aren't as they seem. So, explore this inkling. Don't hide from it.
No matter where this exploration takes you, you'll be on the right track."

May these poems support the exploration of that inkling.

"And as imagination bodies forth
The forms of things unknown, the poet's pen
Turns them to shapes, and gives to airy nothing
A local habitation and a name."

–William Shakespeare, *A Midsummer Night's Dream*

contents

water

air

fire

essence

Introduction

Each of these poems represents an element of the inside-in understanding that I have immersed myself in over the last few years, and a lifetime of learning. None of them are a complete picture, and they all represent my own ever-shifting seeing. They can be read in any order, with no prior understanding.

I've been touched, pulling this collection together, as I hear the message of each poem as though for the first time. And it is a simple message. A message of exploration for its own sake. A message of the recognition of our true nature as love, freedom, peace, joy, beauty, and abundance. A message that starts to inform our everyday lives. We live more in alignment with the love that we are. Bit by bit, ego is cleaned up. We feel less separate. Sure, habitual thoughts will still arise. We might still feel anxious, angry, or hurt. But the more we know these feelings are not our identity, the shallower their roots.

This exploration points away from therapy, techniques,

models, and beliefs and toward the core of experience. It points to what is, beyond judgments, perceptions, sensations, and feelings. It points to the only thing we can ever know for sure, that we are aware. And in awareness, we find the love, freedom, peace, joy, beauty, and abundance we have always been. Right here, right now. A wonderful exploration.

These writings come from the heart, not the head. Let love speak to love.

With Love,

Sara

London, 11 August 2018

earth

A Love Letter to Myself

Dear me,

I knew my "job" for the weekend was to love everyone in the room, including you. I didn't know if that could happen. It felt elusive.

It's as though every thought creates two universes. One where that thought happened, one where it didn't.

It seemed I had reached a dead end, a crisis point. Then, all the universes collapsed back into one universe. In a moment outside time, where all possibilities are true at once. I "bridged" to a universe where that dead end never happened, and love was much more obvious to me. The "job" arose from that moment.

I knew I loved everyone within seconds of entering the room. With brutal honesty, apart from you. I didn't run away. I stayed with that absence. In the middle, without shame. Stayed with all the possible universes.

Late on the second day, the question was asked, "Are you 100 percent OK?" All the universes collapsed into one again, and I fell in love with all the possible yous at once. Every possible past you, every possible future you–every single one. And I found the answer, "100 percent."

I can't not love you now. Experience might show up angry, sad, confused, happy, confident, shaky–but I can't not love you.

I didn't fall into love for that you, in that universe, in that moment of time. I met you in the Now, in the space of infinite possibilities.

And even these words don't quite do it justice. The perfect words elude me. The perfect words are not possible. Love is beyond the words.

Love you.

Be. You.

The simplest two words.
Seen for what they are in an instant.
And a lifetime of stripping away everything that isn't You.
For no reason than the Being of it.

Putting Myself Outside

Putting myself outside
The thought I am this body
Out in the world

Putting you outside
The thought you are not me
Separation

Feeling the thought of me
Shake, crack, crumble to dust
See no outside

No, It's Not OK

No, it's not OK
When you speak to me like that.
No, it's not OK
That you don't hear behind my words.
No, it's not OK
To move the goalposts again.
No, it's not OK
To refuse me space to change.
No, it's not OK
To assume I'll understand.
No, it's not OK
That you don't want to forgive.
No, it's not OK
But I'm OK
And you're OK
And it's OK that we feel like this today.

Differences

They say how great it is we had the serious talk
That we worked out our differences
Put them behind us

What they don't see is there were no differences
Nothing to work out

No investigation of right and wrong
No full and frank exchange of hurts
No redefining boundaries

Simply an eternity between two thoughts
Where subject and object collapsed
Knowing we were one

Impossible

There are times when it all seems impossible.
When there's no way to a draw,
Or even to an honorable defeat.

And all there is to hold on to is the faint whisper,
   "You are Love"–to which the only reasonably polite
   answer is, "Go away."

But the faintest echo says, simply, "Love."
That seems possible.
Even from here.
To be open to love.
Knowing it is not the easy choice.
Knowing life this raw, this vulnerable, this real,
   does not offer any free passes.

From here, love is not perfect but possible.
Right now, possible is enough.

Live It

I am angry. He annoyed me.

I am happy. I feel connected to everyone and everything.

I lose myself. No need for connection,
because I am everything. The stuff it is all made of.

And repeat.

Misunderstanding, understanding, the disintegration of both.

And live it.

Remember

I can't forget that you are me
That any harsh word
Any something
Belongs to me
As much as you

When one of us knows
That there are not two of us
And one of us remembers
Who we are

There is nothing
To forgive
Never was

There is everything
To live
Perfect

Known

In learning
that nothing exists
outside of Consciousness,
nothing is lost.
Everything is just as it was.
But known.
Known in the full,
delicious,
messy beauty
of awareness.

Within

You've heard it, right? "Look within"?
Did they point you to where "within" lies?

It's not found in the human brain, gut, heart or mind.
It's not found on a map.
It's not found through seeking.

"Within" reveals itself in experience.
At the core of experience is the source of experience.
Pure awareness.

Because

I can't not love
Even when something
feels unkind

I can't not love
Even when something
Feels . . .
No
It is not despite the feeling
But simply because

All Shall Be Well

"... all shall be well, and all shall be well, and all manner of
thing shall be well."
–Julian of Norwich

This refrain has been echoing in my mind the last few days.

What does it mean?

It's not promising an easy life.

It's pointing to something more. A background OK-ness, even
as the foreground erupts.

I am angry and hurting. And all shall be well.
I am scared and worrying. And all shall be well.
We will win or lose. And all shall be well.
We will age and die. And all shall be well.

All shall be well. All is well. Even when it isn't.

It can't not be.

I Am

I am angry.
I am happy.
I am insecure.
I am one hundred percent OK.

I am movement. I am stillness.
I am constantly changing thought.
I am constant Love.

I am that I am.

I Am.

Lose Your "Why"

Don't choose your "why"
Lose your "why"

You don't need a "why"
You are the "why"
Already
Life living out perfectly
One with you

Body

Every day, I experience my body
as though it were a solid thing.
Something existing beyond experience.
The human mind naturally looking to the body for answers,
Brilliantly forgetting that it and the body
are perfect expressions of the same source.

Look again, and tell me how anything can exist
beyond experience, beyond awareness, beyond source.

Then live it.

Meeting Point

I am
the impossible meeting point

Where the impossibility of time
dissolves into
eternity

Where the impossibility of space
dissolves into
infinity

Where the impossibility of matter
dissolves into
pure
unbounded
nothing

Where the impossibility of ego
dissolves into
awareness

I am

Flint

If I thought anything,
I thought this understanding
would smooth my edges,
polish me.

Turns out I'm not a rough gemstone,
but a flint.
A flint cracked open.
Jagged, raw.
A weapon.
A cutting Love.

Child of This Land

When I walk
The streets of London
My long-dead grandmother
Walks with me
The ghost of her city
Overlaying mine

When I watch
A Beatle singing
"Let it be" in Liverpool
The Scouse grandfather
I never met
Sings too

When I climb
the hills of Edinburgh
The ghosts of past me
Come too
Memories
At every corner

When I stroll
The English lanes
And leafy forests
My childhood dog
Runs with me
Forever young

I used to say I was
A child of this land
And yearn for it
When far away
But now I know
I can't not be Home

water

The Question Dissolves

Who am I?
There's no me
That I can find
Not tucked
In the recesses
Of what I call
My mind
Nor curled
In my body
Or hidden
In the scribble
Of my name

Who am I?
Freed
From the confines
Of mind
And body
And name
That could never
Contain
Who we are

Seeing
This mind
This body
This name

Are not
Containers
Or limitations
But refractions
Of who we are

Who am I?

There is no one
To ask
And no answers
Needed

The question

Dissolves

Lost

Lost in a sea of words
Lost in waves of complexity
Lost in tides of description
That can never be pinned down

Noticing
I am the ocean
Words dissolve
Complexity untangles
Descriptions soften and blur
No longer lost
Never lost

All In

Living it all in.

I say it so often.
What does it mean?

Is it:
Traveling the world?
Writing books?
Leading events?
Earning money?
Being a superstar?

Maybe "living it all in" isn't:
Sneaking onto the golf course,
Wearing a blanket,
Crying in the soft rain,
Walking barefoot in wet clover,
Drinking coffee under the oak.

But, right now, it feels like it.
All in, nothing on it.

Building Sandcastles

Building sandcastles
Of angry words
And hurt feelings

But sandcastles are only sand
However well built

The incoming tide
Can return them
To what they were made of

Just sand

I Cried

I cried this morning
for the child who thought it was all on her.
I cried this morning
for the girl who tried so hard to be worthy.
I cried this morning
for the young woman who felt all alone.
I cried this morning
for the woman who saw without knowing.

I held each one in my heart.
I cried for each of them.
And let them go.

No Words

The stillness inside
Sweeps the words away
As a gentle tide sometimes
Or now a raging tsunami
Not just emptying the glass
But ripping it from the hand
Shattering into a million pieces

Shattered into a million pieces
The idea of me
Not empty
But gone

No words.

Wave

At your essence
You are the wave
Experiencing itself

The Gift

A metaphor: "Give a man a fish, and you feed him for a day. Teach a man to fish, and you feed him for a lifetime."

A kind teacher helps a student see their story more clearly. It's a warm embrace. A relief.

But, it's a false relief. The student will be hungry again tomorrow.

A brave teacher creates a space for the student to realize they are not their story, and more, who they truly are does not know the story. From pure Consciousness, everything is beautiful and perfect, including the story.

A single insight, a shared experience of One Being–that will feed the student for a lifetime, whatever the story. And more, the student is no longer a student but a fellow explorer.

This is the greatest gift of a teacher. To know who we are already, and to wait there for us.

And to be a reminder of the truth we have always known, the truth that we are.

Soft (Dawn Walks at Sea 1)

The softening of the dawn sky
Watching alone
Briefly thought the whole show
For me–but no
I am here that the dawn
Might be experienced
I am, right here, right now
The experience
Of those smoky tendrils

Walking (Dawn Walks at Sea 2)

When a human walks, it shows up at the back of the
pelvis as a beautiful, constantly redrawn infinity symbol.

It follows, then, that at the heart of the movement
is a point of perfect, infinite stillness.

Sunrise (Dawn Walks at Sea 3)

At times, me walking, watching my second-chance sunrise
   break through the clouds. The very human desire to keep it
   tight, to bottle it and sip it slowly. Sadness at its transience.

Then, a moment of what a wise man once called "paddling
   in the shallows of Consciousness"–a collapsing of subject
   and object, an experience of golden peace at the heart of
   the movement.

And then, walking, smiling, wrapped in the memory of being
   sunrise. And, more than that, the echo of the space
   in which sunrise is held but not known.

Raging (Dawn Walks at Sea 4)

Last night
Ego raging
The idea of me
Raggedy and raw
Feet stamping

This morning
The softening of dawn
A warm caress
Movement flowing
Not from the feet
But from that infinite point
Of perfect stillness

The rising sun
Reflected in my veins
As liquid gold
A cleansing fire

Awareness (Dawn Walks at Sea 5)

Perfect Awareness

Joy unbounded
Freedom unlimited
Love unfettered

Awareness of running

Joy, bounded
Freedom, limited
Love, fettered

Aware of me

Bounded–feeling judged
Limited–pulling my stride
Fettered–fearing not being enough

Turn into the wind
Breath taken away
Joy, Freedom, Love
Found in the space between thoughts

All perfect

Pain (Dawn Walks at Sea 6)

Today, physical pain
Pulling at my heels

First, old patterns
Protecting, cosseting

Then, without prompting
Moving to the heart of the pain

And finding not the sufferer
But the sunrise

New (Dawn Walks at Sea 7)

New dawn
New day
New world

Redrawn every moment
Always Now
Always home

Felt (Dawn Walks at Sea 8)

Something felt
No words

Being (Dawn Walks at Sea 9)

Being
Awareness
The space
In which
All this
Happens

Not known
But held
The space
Of infinite
Possibilities
Where everything
Is Now

air

Thoughts and Storms

Thoughts and storms.
Thought storm.
Sandstorm.
Sand being whipped up, wrapping the air.
Creating the appearance
Of a self
To experience
The storm.

And then.
Blown through.
Leaving the space
That was always here.

Flint and Feather

As far as gravity is concerned, there is no
difference between a flint stone and a feather.
In a vacuum, released together, they'd
hit the ground together.
Which reminds me of some rainy afternoons
in a student house,
with weights from the kitchen scales, a
stopwatch and a very tall stairwell.
I digress.

As far as gravity is concerned, there is no
difference between a flint stone and a feather.
Yet, sensation tells me otherwise.
In my hand, the flint is still warm from the sun.
Solidly here.
I feel it all. The rough, rounded side. The
smooth sharp side.
The feather, though, rests in my hand so lightly,
I don't feel it.
I close my eyes; it may as well not be there.

As far as gravity is concerned, there is no
difference between a flint stone and a feather.

The Present Moment

The constant hunt
For the present moment
A place to reach
A nirvana within time

And yet
The palest reflection
Of the full power
Of the single Moment
Once and forever
An undivided Now
Outside of time

Gently cradling
Every possible moment
Every past
Every future

One Being
Holding every possible experience
Like a grain of sand
In the palm of the hand
And that grain containing universes

Every possible moment
Dissolving into Now

Midsummer Sun

Chasing the midsummer sun
Suspended in a bubble of time
The hands on the clock are stilled
Drifting in a landscape of clouds

English Country Lanes

English country lanes
Walking me home

There is nothing to be taught
And no one to teach

I am the soft morning sky
I am the birdsong

All of it, none of it
Always home

Walk Gently in the Fields of Time

Walk gently in the fields of time, my dear
Meander through the years
Among the rows of hours and minutes
Like neatly planted wheat

Feel the seconds ripple as grains
Between your fingers

Rest in the long, soft grasses
And dream of misty futures

Walk gently in the fields of time, my dear

Who Am I?

Who am I?
I am what is thought.
And who am I
Between thoughts?
Everything.

Recognized

In imagination only
But not my imagination
For I am imagined

In sensation only
But not my senses
For I am felt

In Consciousness only
But not my consciousness
For I am experienced

In realization only
Made real
And recognized

Thought

Thought
Ethereal
Ephemeral
Like a whispered word
Or a kiss in the dark
To be experienced
Not held

Perception

A shift in perception is not a new way
of looking at the same world.
A shift in perception is to see before the world.
To its source.
To see, for a moment outside of time, how flimsy is
everything that looked so solid.
And to find, instead, something permanently reliable.
From there, we come back to a new world.

Glimpse

For the
Briefest
Of moments

I heard
What is
Before hearing

I saw
What is
Before sight

I felt
What is
Before touch

And I was all of it.

That single
Undivided
Glimpse

Is enough

More than
Enough
For
All time

A life lived
In the forgetting
And the remembering

Imperfectly
Perfectly
So

What I Say

Here's what I say:
"He annoyed me"
"I am sad that she is sick"
"I worry about my job"

Here's what is real:
I am annoyed
I am sad
I am worried

Here's what is beyond:
I am Freedom
I am Love
I am Joy

A perpetual dance. I am all of it.

Creation Song

Consciousness sings
A song of creation
Beauty beyond words

A song so powerful
Objects are birthed
And dance and die in it

All life springs forth
And dissolves
Not known, but held

And the harmony soars on
Echoing in whale song
And the wind in the trees

Reflected in a baby's first cry
Angry words, soft kisses
Shared silence

All loved

All perfect

All You

Do You Pray?

Do you pray?
Do you ask the universe?
Do you wish?

Could you pray for only love, peace, wisdom, freedom, joy?
Would you give up on every personal thing you pray for?

That's you touching true nature.
Which is love, peace, wisdom, freedom and joy.

Between Two Thoughts

I've died a million deaths
In the eternal space
Between two thoughts

Disappeared into nothing
Lost all idea of me
Then found myself again

Like a star collapsing
And being reborn
Back at the beginning of time

Rising

Rising
I battle
I fight
I struggle
I manage
I cope
I control
I handle
I fix.

Resting
I am.

Knowing

Knowing who you are.
Knowing the normality of all of it.
Of feeling insecure, then knowing that insecurity is OK.
Of feeling Love, and knowing Love is utterly ordinary.
Of the perpetual dance between insecurity and Love.
Of knowing life to be a dream of Consciousness,
and, gloriously, living it.

It's the Most Natural Thing

It's the most natural thing
To fall asleep

And for dreams to come
Bringing dragons and battles
And monsters
And puppies that turn
Into parrots
And complex challenges
Like turning parrots
Into puppies
To save humankind
And houses that shape-shift
So I can never find a room
And sand dunes to climb
With worn-out limbs
The top always just out of reach
And my closest friends
Kicking sand in my face

It's the most natural thing
To wake

In waking
Dreams dissolve
Like morning mist
The parrots turn back
Into puppies
And run off to frolic
With the dragons
In gentle sand dunes
And the monsters vanish
Back under the bed
And the battles
No longer need fighting
And my friends are the Love
They always were

And I don't need to save humankind

fire

The Fire Burns

The fire burns bright
And shadows dance

The dancing shadows
Just a pale reflection
Of the flame

If not for the fire
There would be no shadows

There are no answers
In the shadows
However enticing the patterns

Shadows no more
Than the absence of light

Look to the flame
Not for answers
But because there's nowhere else to look

The fire burns bright
The shadows subside

Head to Heart

As strangers
We stood close
For a moment
I fell out of my head
And into my heart

And more
Ego dissolved
Into Awareness
Beyond time
We were Love

I opened my eyes
And there was
Only you and me
In that moment
I fell in love with you

Fear

To the one who fears:
it's not
the thing
you fear
it's not
the thought of
the thing
you fear
it's not
"that" you think
creating fear
for you to feel
there is no you
beyond the fear
you are what is thought

Haiku: The Eternal Dance of Life

Formless into form
The eternal dance of life
Form into formless

Create to destroy
The eternal dance of life
Destroy to create

Knowing the unknown
The eternal dance of life
Unknowing the known

Ego Rages

Ego rages against anything that threatens it.
Silence and stillness threaten ego.
Silence–not the absence of noise, but beyond noise.
Stillness–not the absence of movement,
but beyond movement.
Ego is only noise and movement.
Creating the idea of separation, the idea of me.
Beyond noise and movement, ego dissolves.
In silence and stillness, there is no ego.

Dancing with Shadows

I was standing
With my back to the sun
Taking photos of shadows
Believing those pictures
Were real

I turned
Was dazzled by the sun
Basked in the light

Enjoying the shadows
For what they are
Dancing with them
Losing myself in them
Loving them

I am the shadows
I am the light
I am

I Think

I say, "I think"
As if "I"
Is best described
By mind

I say, "I'm in my head"
As if "I"
Is best described
By body

But . . .

But I also know
And can't undo the knowing
That answers are not found
In mind or body
Any more than in shadows
On the wall of a cave

"So what?" you ask.
So what, indeed.
Just so.

I Lost Myself

I lost myself in the sunset.
I lost myself in your eyes.
I lost myself in that game.
I lost myself in a book.

I lost myself.
Nothing more.

The briefest of moments,
With no idea of "me."
Nothing veiling
Pure Love,
Pure Freedom,
Pure Awareness.

Lake Sunset

There are times when there are no words.
In intimacy and silence, our true nature is apparent,
And words dissolve into love.

Inside Out

When I first heard the term "inside out," it sounded much the
same as "upside down" or "back to front."

Simply something at odds with what the world
has expressed.

A gift to me because, upside down, it all made sense.

A gateway to who I truly am.

Dance–Sing–Love–Live

We are the dancing, the singing,
the loving and the living.
Activity in perpetual motion.
At the heart of the movement,
there is no one to do it.

Realizing this, we see who we truly are:

One Dance, wild and unbridled;
One Song, soaring and strong;
One Love, perfect and whole;
One Being, God undivided.

Realizing this, we live it.

The Dance flowing into the dancing.
The Song flowing into the singing.
Love, raw and open.
One Being experiencing it all.

Heaven on earth, even when it doesn't feel like it.

Where Do I End?

I ask myself, where do I end?
Can it be where my feet touch the earth?
Or the sound of birdsong reaches my ears?
Or the sight of you reaches my eyes?

Yet, I sense no boundary.
Like mapping a coastline
In ever increasing levels of detail
The closer I look
The further I get from a definitive measure.

What if I abandon that quest?
And ask instead–if I am all of this, what then?

So What?

I'm not what I think about
So what?

I'm not what I think
So what?

I'm not the thinker
Now you've got my interest

Tell me more
If not that, then who?

This Love

This love, raw and open
This love, wild and unbridled
This love, soaring and strong
This love, perfect and whole

This love cannot be hurt
Yet cries with me
This love has never lost
Yet bathes my wounds
This love knows no limit
Yet holds my heart

This love lives me
This love is me

Choice

Tell me, if you truly had free choice,
are there not things you'd change?

I have tried and tried.
To change myself.
To change others.
To change situations.
Failed and suffered.
Over and over.

If there was a choice,
I'd have chosen differently.
Yet, it turns out,
Belief in choice is simply
Another resistance to what is.

Resistance blew itself up,
Burned itself out.
In its absence,
The realization of what is.

In realizing what is,
There was no need
To make it different.
Even if that were possible.

Naturally,
Resistance rises again.
And burns itself out again.
And again.

In the heart of the experience
Lies an invitation to what always is.
What we are.
Love.
Regardless of circumstances.
Regardless of mood.
Regardless of thought.

Forgiveness

Beyond the concept of forgiveness
Is a love that burns away every thought
About myself, you and the world.
Leaving only pure awareness.
Leaving nothing to forgive.
No one to be forgiven.
And no one to do the forgiving.

Consciousness

Consciousness is a Love so raw, so powerful, so real, so strong.
A Love that knows who I am, without exception or omission.
A Love that calls me home on the wild and stormy nights.
This Love burns.

It burns away the need to be the nice,
quiet, clever, good, helpful girl.
It burns away the excuses about not being enough.
I've never been more certain of who I am, nor so confused.
This Love leaves no choices.

essence

Seeking

The act of seeking cannot know itself,
It can only act.
In the heart of the seeking
There is no one there to seek
And nothing to be sought.

Separation

The language of separation is so prevalent,
we hardly even notice it.

But it speaks to the activity of separation and
suggests a being that can be separate.
From Self. From God.

If we speak of a distinction between you and me,
we suggest a differentiation between you and You.

And that which sees separation is lost.

you IS You, we are One. Never separate.
The shared experience of this is never lost.

Now What?

You are pure Awareness,
experiencing itself in the world–now what?

Learning

In learning
We seek
To acquire

In understanding
We see clearly
Pure awareness

Aware of being aware
Of boundless freedom
And limitless love

Love

How do we explain Love?
We don't

If it has an explanation
It's not Love

If it needs an explanation
It's not Love

Home

Home can be as simple as a quiet feeling of OK-ness,
Or as dramatic as a bolt from the blue.

Home has no location in time, space or matter.
It is not found in the human body or mind.

We rest at Home, always, Here and Now.
Home is our true nature, and we can never be lost.

Love Alone

Love,
dissolving sensation.

Love,
shining through perception.

Love,
quieting thought.

Love,
sweeping away objections.

Love,
obliterating separation.

Love,
calling me home.

Love,
alone, perfect, magnificent.

Love.

When You Know

When you know yourself as love,
that knowing will express itself as love.

When you know yourself as peace,
that knowing will express itself as peace.

When you know yourself as freedom,
that knowing will express itself as freedom.

Rest

Rest, my dear, rest here.
Find, beyond noise and movement,
Stillness and silence

No Possessions

A mind
Does not
Have wisdom
For a mind
Is the idea
Of separation
And an idea
Has no possessions

Quietness

There is a quietness that
   pervades my experience.
Asserts itself above the cacophony
   of raging thought storms.
Offers permanence,
   in the center of change.
Offers stillness,
   in the center of movement.

Pure Knowing

Pure knowing.
Nothing to be done with it.
No meaning to be given to it.

Pure knowing.
No personal benefit.
Nothing personal.
No personal.

Pure knowing.
Showing up in experience.
Informing experience.
Is experience.

Pure knowing.
Even when it looks like it isn't.
And the stuff that feels so solid
Is "made" of exactly that same pure knowing.
Experienced as real only by an
apparent limitation of that same knowing.
Created by thought. Apparent limitation.
Experienced as real.
Until it isn't.

Pure knowing.
So simple.
Words are not enough.

Speaking Love in the World

In the silence
In the gaps
Between words

Between thoughts
Of me
And the world

Love
Needs
No qualifier

Awareness
Needs
No explanation

Yet words
Return
With me

To share
What I
Remember

Speaking of
Pure Love
In the world

When Time Stands Still

When time stands still
Eternity catches us unaware
Takes our feet out from under us
Brings us to our knees
Fills us to overflowing with awe and wonder

Then we blink
The world rushes back in
And continues just like normal
But forever changed

One Infinite Being

In pure Love, pure Awareness
We look out at the world
And see ourself everywhere.
We see our one infinite Being
In everyone and everything
Reflected back at us, as us
This is Home

Come With Me

Come with me
She whispered
And held out her hand

Yes, he said
Let me pack
Tidy up, say goodbye

No, she said
Now. Right now
There is only now

He nodded
And she smiled
As they disappeared

Light

The singular reality
Of Love
Is the light by which
All its apparent objects
Are known.

The Search Stops Here

And

if

who

we

are

is

what

is

sought

the search stops here

With thanks to:

Richard
Joel
Garret
Team IO 2018
And all at Greenleaf

About the Author

Sara Priestley brings a fresh new voice to poetry, blending ancient spiritual traditions with reflections on everyday experience. She is a longtime explorer of true nature, having earned degrees in theology and information technology, accompanied by studies in psychology and physiology. With clarity, lightness, and simplicity, Sara shares profound truths. Though Sara's approach to poetry is often described as an inside-out way of knowing, she prefers to call it *inside-in*, to bring recognition to the directness of the paths of understanding.

Sara teaches this inside-in understanding via social media, at retreats, in workshops, and on video coaching calls (usually accompanied by Pretzel the cat). She lives with her husband, and just the perfect number of cats, in London, England. Readers can email Sara with questions or comments at sara@livinglifesideways.co.uk.

Made in the USA
Middletown, DE
24 March 2019